THE THOUGHTS OF CHAIRMAN MIAOW

ANDREW DAVIES

GRAMERCY BOOKS
NEW YORK

© 2005 PRC Publishing Limited,
The Chrysalis Building,
Bramley Road, London W10 6SP

An imprint of **Chrysalis** Books Group plc

This 2005 edition is published by Gramercy Books, an imprint of
Random House Value Publishing, a division of Random House, Inc.,
New York, by arrangement with Chrysalis Books, London.

Gramercy is a registered trademark and the colophon is a trademark
of Random House, Inc.

Random House
New York • Toronto • London • Sydney • Auckland
www.randomhouse.com

Printed and bound in Malaysia

A catalog record for this title is available from the Library of Congress.

ISBN 0-517-22599-9

10 9 8 7 6 5 4 3 2 1

IN RECENT YEARS

there have been many negative things written about Chairman Miaow and the political changes he has brought about to transform the most populous nation on earth. It has not been easy for Miaow in his struggle to bring freedom to the pussycat proletariat. He has had to educate and inform illiterate peasants, left ignorant by feudalist paper tigers and their imperialist cohorts because it suited them.

Miaow's journey has been a long one. If you thought *Incredible Journey* by Walt Disney was long, this one is three times longer. And

WE MUST HAVE FAITH
IN THE PARTY AND WE MUST HAVE FAITH IN
MOIST POUCHES

also, with no annoying dogs. As Miaow once told us, a journey of 1000 miles begins with a single leap into the bushes. After many years of struggle we have made this great leap forward.

Chairman Miaow's revolutionary party is based on Marxist-Leninist political theory. It is impossible to lead the working classes, the moggy masses, our kitten comrades, without educating them with the values and goals of this theory.

To inform the masses, to educate them and illuminate their lives with the beauty of Marxist-Leninism, Miaow has ordered many posters and slogans to be created that demonstrate the values of our future nation. These posters have also been used to expose the rabid rantings and evil influences of President Woof and purge his decadent doggy influence from our society.

SCRATCHING A CHAIR IS THE HIGHEST FORM OF STRUGGLE FOR RESOLVING CONTRADICTIONS

Much of this work has been done by a dedicated team of artists who have slaved tirelessly and with little reward to produce posters that will inspire the population. They are true heroes and Miaow salutes their glorious efforts.

This special publication draws together many of the great political posters that Miaow has inspired, created for him by his loyal subjects. It shows correct behavior by the people, it shows Miaow's forces triumphing over the evil President Woof and the toadying Prime Minister Ruff, it shows heroic workers engaged in the production of iron, steel, energy, and baskets. It is the proof, if any proof were needed, that Miaow rubs his head against the legs of no one to achieve his goals. It shows that Miaow's victory is utter and complete, and that his influence will last long into the 21st century as a shining example to us all.

LONG LIVE
CHAIRMAN MIAOW!

MIAOW SAYS

STUDY REVOLUTIONARY THEORY.

BURN DOWN THE EDIFICES OF CAPITALISM, THEN HAVE A LONG NAP IN A WARM SPOT.

IT IS GOOD TO HAVE JUST ONE KITTEN.

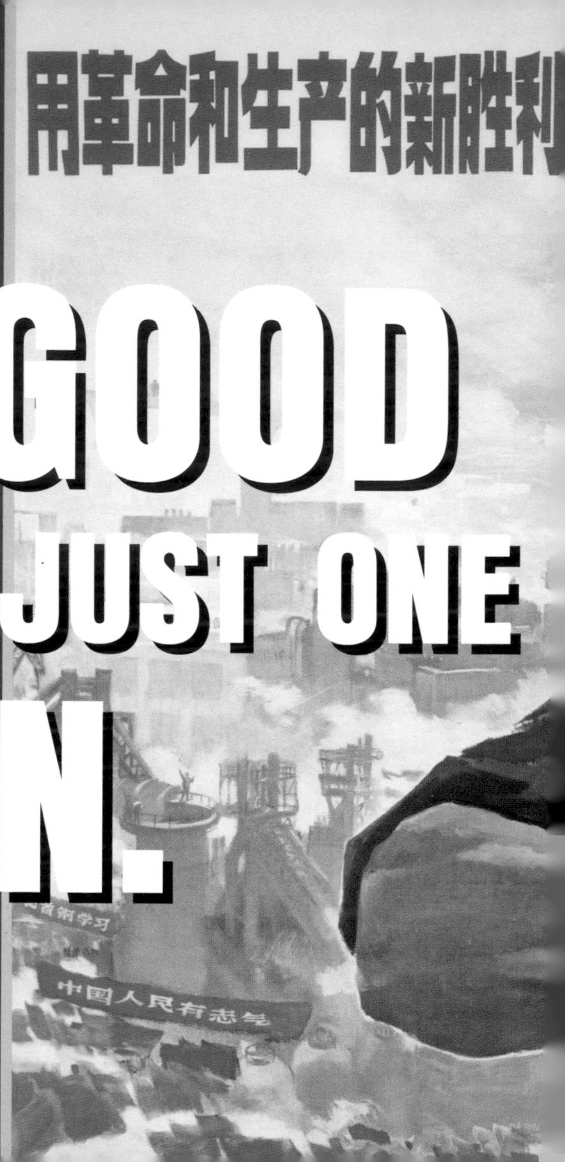

YOU CAN ALSO USE MIAOW'S
LITTLE RED BOOK
TO MAKE NOTES OF IMPORTANT
REVOLUTIONARY ACTIVITIES, SUCH AS
STREET PARTIES
AND WORMING.

DARE TO THINK, DARE TO ACT, DARE TO PUT ON MUSICALS.

WE MUST HAVE FAITH
THAT THE PEASANT MASSES ARE
READY TO ADVANCE STEP BY STEP
ALONG THE ROAD OF SOCIALISM AND
PAY FOR CAT LITTER.

A HUNDRED FLOWERS BLOOM

COMMIAOWNISTS
ARE LIKE SEEDS AND THE
MASSES ARE LIKE THE SOIL.

TOGETHER WE WILL
ENJOY A GLORIOUS
MARXIST-LENINIST
HARVEST FESTIVAL.

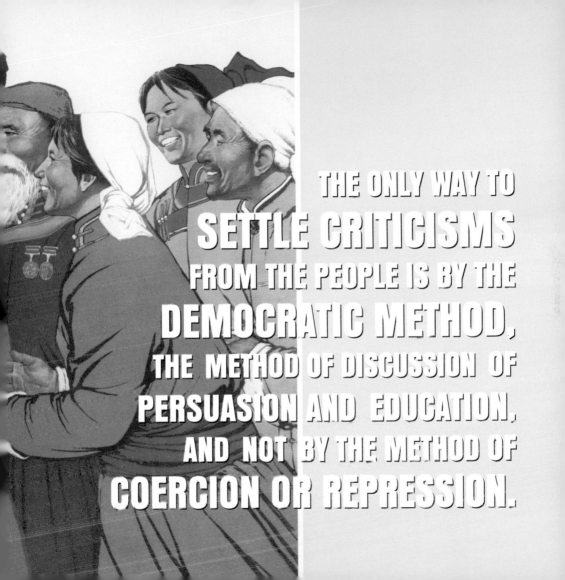

THE ONLY WAY TO **SETTLE CRITICISMS** FROM THE PEOPLE IS BY THE **DEMOCRATIC METHOD,** THE METHOD OF DISCUSSION OF **PERSUASION AND EDUCATION,** AND NOT BY THE METHOD OF **COERCION OR REPRESSION.**

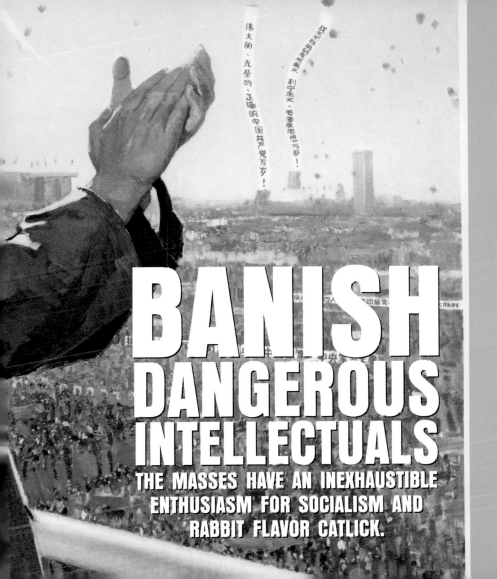

BANISH
DANGEROUS
INTELLECTUALS

**THE MASSES HAVE AN INEXHAUSTIBLE
ENTHUSIASM FOR SOCIALISM AND
RABBIT FLAVOR CATLICK.**

COMRADES!

BEWARE MEXICAN COUNTER-REVOLUTIONARIES AND WOOFISH PUPPETS TIPPING RICE IN YOUR EAR.

MIAOW SAYS

THE PEOPLE'S DAILY USED CORRECTLY
IS AS POWERFUL AS A GUN OR A GRENADE.

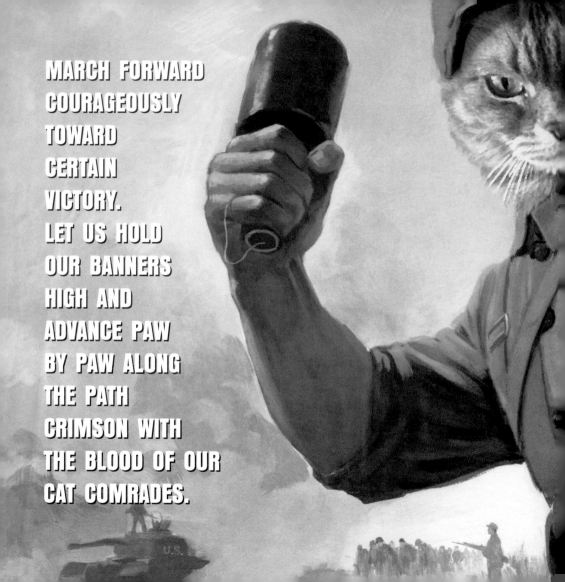

LONG LIVE
CHAIRMAN MIAOW
DEATH TO
PRESIDENT WOOF!

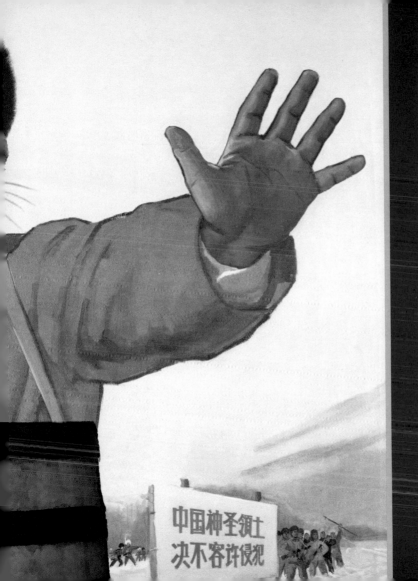

POLITICAL POWER

GROWS OUT OF A BARREL OF FISH.

中国神圣领土
决不容许侵犯

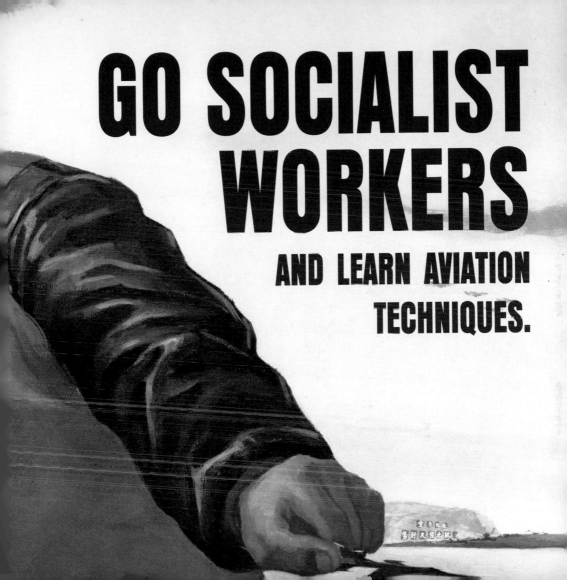

PRACTICE SELF-CRITICISM

IS IMPERIALIST FILM
OFFICER AND
A GENTLEMAN
REALLY SO COOL...?

AND SUPPORT THE GLORIOUS EFFORTS OF THE

PUSSYCAT LIBERATION ARMY.

ACHIEVE THE FOUR MODERNIZATIONS

NEW RADIO, NEW FURNITURE, SNAPPY SOCKS, AND GREAT HOME DECOR.

EMANCIPATE THE MIND, **FOCUS** ON GOALS, **EMBRACE** THE MASSES, MAKE YOUR EYEBROWS LOOK ANGRY, SHOUT A LOT. **SUPPORT** MIAOW UNITED!

MIAOW HAS TOLD US,

ANY PROPER PARTY

NEEDS TWO CRATES
OF CATNIP AND
SOME FIT KITTIES.

毛主席语录

让哲学从哲学家的课堂上和节本里解放出来，变为群众手里的尖锐武器。

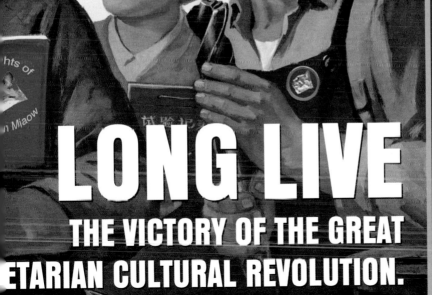

认真学习毛主席的哲学著作！

千万不要忘记阶级斗争！

LONG LIVE

THE VICTORY OF THE GREAT
ETARIAN CULTURAL REVOLUTION.

DO NOT EMBRACE REVISIO

MARXIST-LENINI

THE FLAG OF MIAOW IS RED WITH THE BLOOD OF SMALL RODENTS THAT HAVE GIVEN THEIR LIVES TO BECOME A LIGHT LUNCH FOR THE WORKERS.

RESPECT
THE PARTY SONG.
SOLDIERS, REMEMBER THAT PLEASURE-SEEKING WITH FOLK GUITARS IS
FORBIDDEN
IN THE RED ARMY.

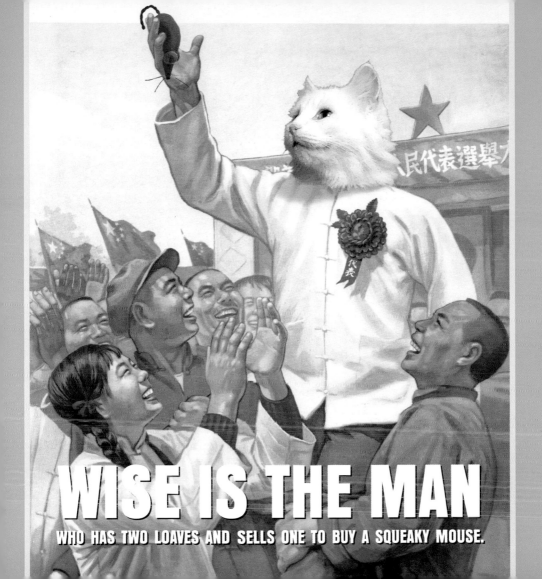

WISE IS THE MAN
WHO HAS TWO LOAVES AND SELLS ONE TO BUY A SQUEAKY MOUSE.

WITH A YOUNG SOCIALIST WORKER'S RAILCARD YOU CAN CONTINUE THE STRUGGLE FOR HALF PRICE AT WEEKENDS.

FIGHT

FAIL, FIGHT AGAIN, FAIL AGAIN, FIGHT AGAIN TILL IMPERIALISM AND THE FORCES OF PRESIDENT WOOF ARE

BANISHED

FROM THE STAGE OF HISTORY.

LINE-DANCING
IS THE HIGHEST FORM OF
STRUGGLE FOR RESOLVING
CONTRADICTIONS.

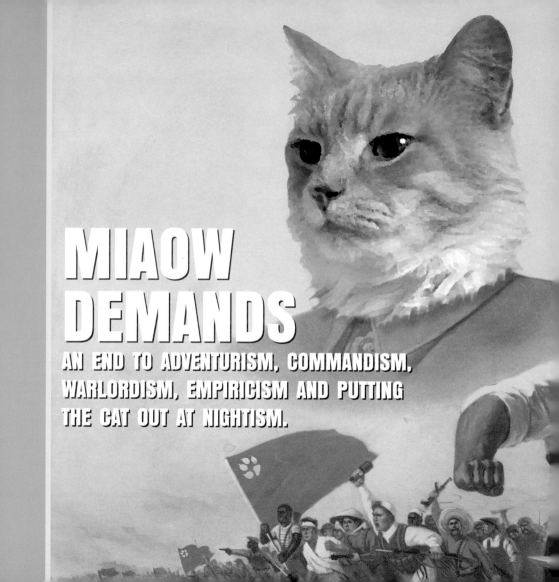

MIAOW
DEMANDS

AN END TO ADVENTURISM, COMMANDISM,
WARLORDISM, EMPIRICISM AND PUTTING
THE CAT OUT AT NIGHTISM.

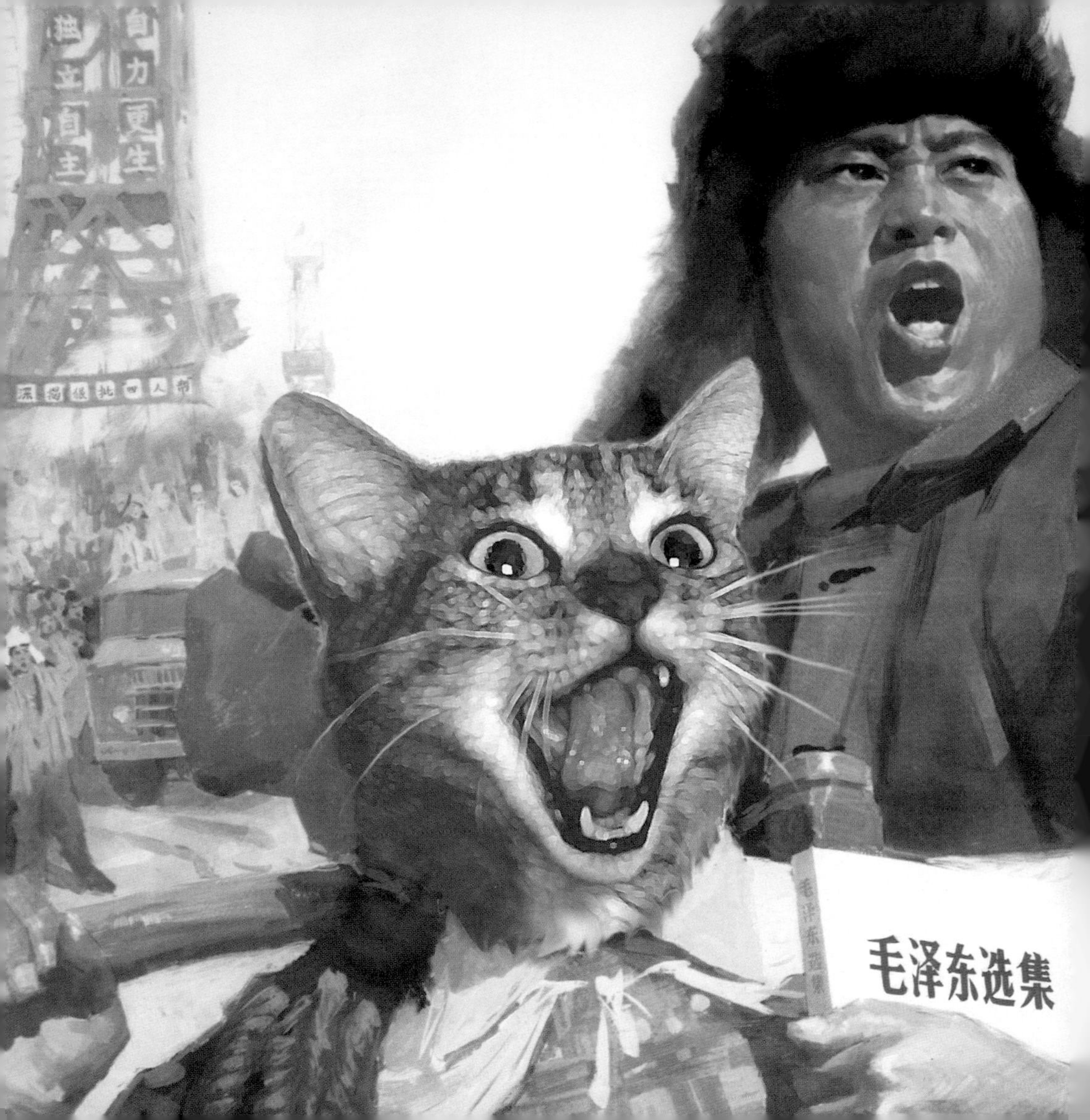
自力更生
独立自主
深揭狠批四人帮
毛泽东选集
毛泽东选集

LET'S SING A NEW SONG ABOUT BANK NATIONALIZATION AND RABBIT FLAVOR CHUNKS.

THE EASIEST WAY TO CATCH A WOOFIAN SPY IS TO THROW A STICK.

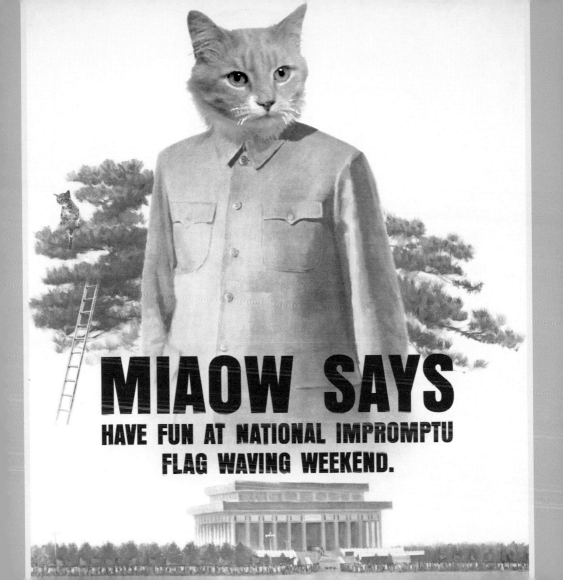

OFFER A BIG HAN
TO OUR EAST EUROPEAN COMMIAOWNIST BRO

OF FRIENDSHIP

S. BUT DO NOT STARE AT THEIR FUNNY CAPS.

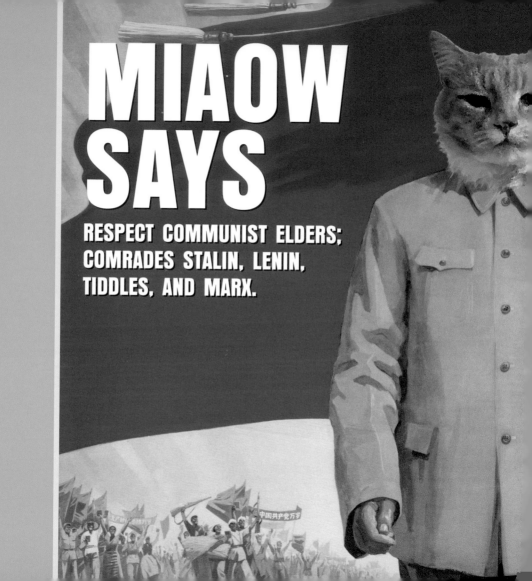

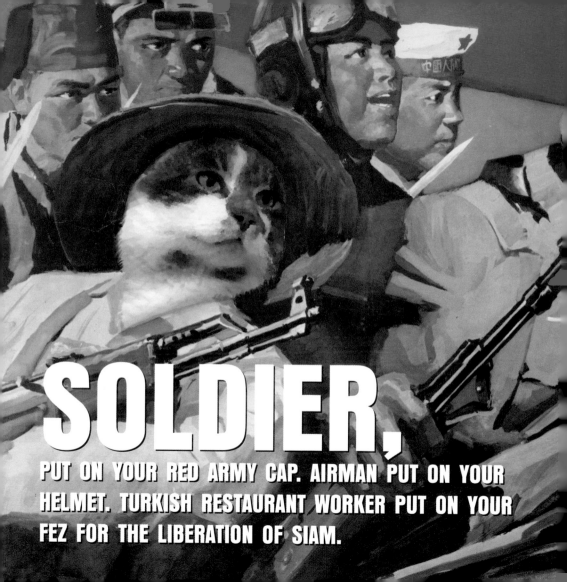

SOLDIER,

PUT ON YOUR RED ARMY CAP. AIRMAN PUT ON YOUR
HELMET. TURKISH RESTAURANT WORKER PUT ON YOUR
FEZ FOR THE LIBERATION OF SIAM.

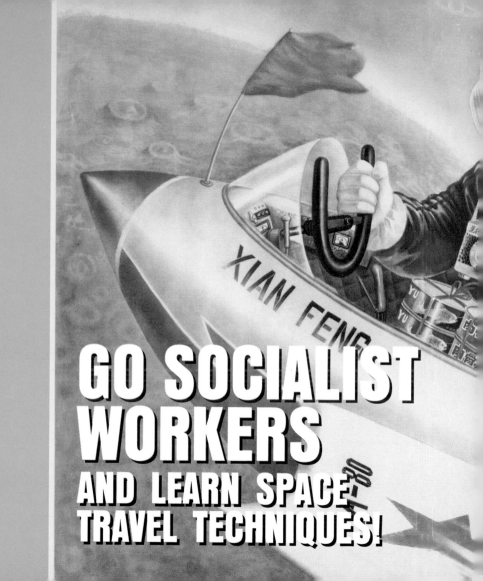

GO SOCIALIST
WORKERS
AND LEARN SPACE
TRAVEL TECHNIQUES!

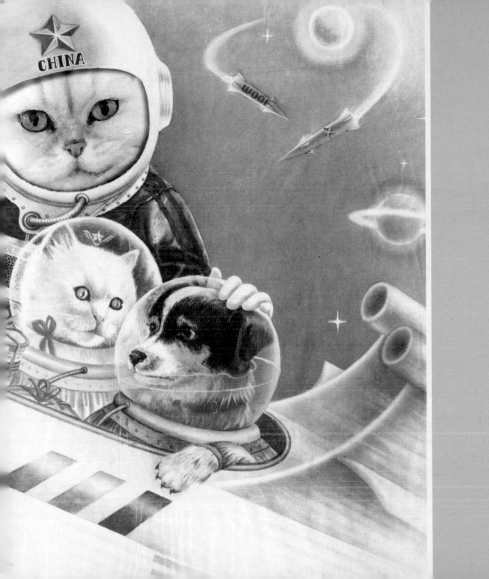

MAKE A TRAIN JOURNEY PASS
IN SECONDS WITH MIAOW'S

BOOK OF GREAT
POLITICAL THOUGHTS.

THOUGHT NO.1
MIAOW MIAOW MIAOW MIAOW. MIAOW
MIAOW MIAOW MIAOW. MIAOW!

MIAOW'S THEORY IS SIMPLE:

中国人民解放军
毛泽东思想宣传队

Thoughts of
Man Miaow

Thoughts of

THE CONTRADICTIONS AMONG THE PEOPLE COMPRISE THE CONTRADICTIONS WITHIN THE WORKING CLASS, THE CONTRADICTIONS WITHIN THE PEASANTRY, THE CONTRADICTIONS WITHIN THE INTELLIGENTSIA, THE CONTRADICTIONS BETWEEN THE WORKING CLASS AND THE PEASANTRY, THE CONTRADICTIONS BETWEEN THE WORKERS AND PEASANTS ON THE ONE HAND AND THE INTELLECTUALS ON THE OTHER, THE CONTRADICTIONS BETWEEN THE WORKING CLASS AND OTHER SECTIONS OF THE WORKING PEOPLE ON THE ONE HAND AND THE NATIONAL BOURGEOISIE ON THE OTHER, THE CONTRADICTIONS BETWEEN MOIST MEATY POUCHES AND DRY, FISH-FLAVORED CAT BISCUITS, AND SO ON. MIAOW'S PUSSYCAT GOVERNMENT SERVES THE PEOPLE. NEVERTHELESS, THERE ARE STILL CERTAIN CONTRADICTIONS BETWEEN THE GOVERNMENT AND THE PEOPLE. THESE INCLUDE CONTRADICTIONS AMONG THE INTERESTS OF THE STATE, THE INTERESTS OF THE COLLECTIVE AND THE INTERESTS OF THE INDIVIDUAL; BETWEEN DEMOCRACY AND CENTRALISM; BETWEEN THE LEADERSHIP AND THE LED; AND THE CONTRADICTION ARISING FROM THE BUREAUCRATIC STYLE OF WORK OF CERTAIN GOVERNMENT WORKERS IN THEIR RELATIONS WITH THE MASSES.

COMRADE KITTENS
BE UNITED, ALERT, EARNEST, AND LIVELY, AND
MOST IMPORTANTLY,
REMEMBER WHICH END OF GUN SHELL GOES IN.

RELY ON
THE WORKING CLASS
WHOLEHEARTEDLY!
BUT BE ALERT TO THE DANGERS
OF WOOFIST TENDENCIES WITHIN.

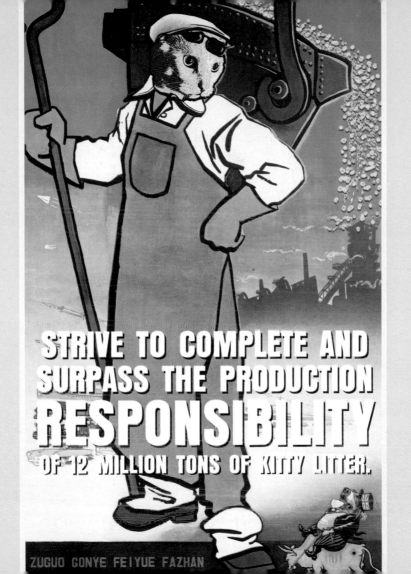

Picture Acknowledgments

Special thanks to Katherine and staff at the Cats Protection North London Homing Centre, for making it possible to photograph comrades Custard, Miso, Pooh, Perkins, Cinders, Hercules, Tizzy, Sabre, Popcorn, Gina and Scruffy.

© Chrysalis Image Library/Eddie MacDonald for all cat portraits.

Collection International Institute of Social History, Amsterdam and the Stefan R. Landsberger Collection at the International Institute of Social History, Amsterdam supplied all of the Chinese propaganda posters in this book.

Photo manipulation and picture effects by David Watts @ www.dwwdesign.com.